WHAT PEOPLE ARE SAYING ABOUT

YOU ARE AWESOME

"If you are a bit nervous or unsure of trying new things, then I think you should read this book and it will help you to try and be awesome!"

—Ethan, age 10

"I have also taken on board some of the advice and think it will help me as well as my son. I would urge every parent to get this book and to learn that everyone can be awesome!"

—Ian (Ethan's dad)

"A must for any parent, I'm learning loads from the Ping-Pong Guy's new book."
—Andrew Flintoff

"I loved this! The book was so inspirational in many ways that I loved, it made me laugh."

—Libby, age 10

"It is for any child who might be feeling that everyone is getting places except them, who doesn't feel good enough, and challenges the thing that holds you back (mostly your own insecurities)."

—Rachel (Libby's mom)

"I think this book is awesome. It is easy to read and very gripping. The things it teaches you are great life skills that can be applied to almost everything."
—William, age 12

"I loved this book. Easy to read and easily relatable. Even my dyslexic son who isn't a fan of reading has read it. It is a page-turner and so positive. It really encourages children to be the best at whatever it is they want to do in life."
—Lindsey (William's mom)

THE

YOU
ARE
AWE
SOME
JOURNAL

For Evie and Teddy. You are still Awesome!

First published in the United States in 2020 by Sourcebooks

Text © 2018, 2020 by Matthew Syed
Illustrations © 2018, 2020 by Toby Triumph and Hodder & Stoughton Ltd.
Cover and internal design © 2020 by Sourcebooks
Images © Shutterstock

Published by Sourcebooks eXplore, an imprint of Sourcebooks Kids
P.O. Box 4410, Naperville, Illinois 60567–4410
(630) 961-3900
sourcebookskids.com

Originally published in 2018 in United Kingdom by Wren & Rook, an imprint of
Hachette Children's Group, part of Hodder & Stoughton.

Library of Congress Cataloging-in-Publication Data is on file with the publisher.

Source of Production: Versa Press, East Peoria, Illinois, USA
Date of Production: October 2020
Run Number: 5020179

Printed and bound in the United States of America.
VP 10 9 8 7 6 5 4 3 2

THE
YOU ARE AWE SOME
JOURNAL

Matthew Syed

ILLUSTRATED BY

Lindsey Sagar
& Toby Triumph

sourcebooks
eXplore

CONTENTS

INTRODUCTION

I HAVE A BIG DENT IN MY HEAD.

It's massive. A crater. Not quite big enough for a table-tennis ball (yes, I've tried) but almost. And it is unfortunate that I don't have much hair, because if we meet, you'll definitely see it. I got it when my brother and I thought it would be a good idea to test whether a magnet would stick to the ceiling of our bedroom in Reading, England. He threw it because he said he was better at throwing than me (debatable), and before I had time to move, it landed on my skull and there was a big hole in my head (not debatable). There was blood everywhere!

WHY ON EARTH AM I TELLING YOU THIS, YOU MIGHT BE ASKING?

Well, it's because the whole fiasco reminded me of how we become Awesome at stuff. And, as you've probably guessed, it's not by trying to lodge a magnet in your brain. But stick with me, I'll get to the point, I promise...

So it turns out that lots of people think you have to be born Awesome. That you come wailing into the world with a bunch of talents and then you're all set. Forever. Destined either for greatness, or not–if you weren't that lucky the day they decided to dish out the good genes for math or tennis or nailing the 720° Gazelle Flip on a skateboard.

But as it happens, that is not why some people are great at things and others are not. And the good news is there is tons you can do to improve your skills at (pretty much) anything. The truth is we get good at stuff by trying new things, making mistakes, and learning what to do better next time. It's all about the effort you're willing to put in, the courage you have to be brave and the resilience you have to do things that are tricky when you first start, but get easier the more often you practice. And if you have read *You Are Awesome* (brilliant book, by the way. Amazing author. Except for his head dent.), you'll already know the secrets of how to get good at the stuff you want to get good at.

Now, we realized three things pretty quickly from the magnet debacle: **(1)** My brother wasn't that good at throwing; **(2)** Magnets don't stick to a ceiling made of green (yes, you read that right) painted plasterboard; and **(3)** I needed to improve my reaction times if I was going to be a world-class table-tennis player (and dodger of falling magnets).

The whole incident was most definitely a mistake. **DO NOT** try this at home. Trust me on that one. But we had tested something new, (completely) failed, and figured out that magnets don't stick to ceilings in suburban Reading, and that we'd better focus on some serious table-tennis practice instead.

So that's what we did. We practiced hard in our garage. And I mean really hard. With anyone who lived near us. It wasn't easy and it didn't happen quickly. It was a journey with lots of mistakes along the way (one of which ended up with a twenty-four-hour international bus trip to the wrong country). Did you know there are two towns called Bergen? (Me neither, but that is a whole other story.) But my brother and I both became Awesome at table tennis. And so did lots of the other kids on my street. If it is all about the talent you're born with, then go figure out how that happened...

So, we know that we can become Awesome. But sometimes getting started on our journey can be hard, and we might need a little bit of help. Everyone needs help. Top sports people have great coaches, brilliant musicians have great teachers, and (I know this will come as a shock) the Kardashians have a lot of help with their hair. So whatever you decide you'd like to become Awesome at, this journal is here to help you figure things out. What should you focus on? How should you even start? What should you practice? How do you cope when things are hard?

So, let's get practical. That's what this journal is all about.

Skip to **Scenario C** opposite if You Are (Already) Awesome and have read the best book ever...okay, that's *Harry Potter and the Goblet of Fire*, but *You Are Awesome* by me, Matthew (dent head) Syed, is maybe worth a read too. If you've got a few spare moments between chores and watching paint dry. Otherwise, start with...

SCENARIO A

Hang on... What on Earth? What do you mean you haven't read it yet? Someone told me it was the greatest and funniest book ever written. Okay, so that was only actually my mom, but after the magnet incident it has taken years to get her in a good mood, so I was quite pleased with her review. And anyway, it is definitely worth a read because it lets you in on the real secrets behind how success really happens. It gives you the inside track and debunks the myth that you need to be born brilliant. And who wouldn't want that?

So head down to the bookshop now. Buy twelve if you want (it's the perfect Christmas gift apparently, or so my agent keeps saying). I'll wait for you while you read it...

Good. You're back. Quicker than I thought. You clearly didn't go on the bus and end up in the wrong country like me (Germany instead of Norway, since you ask). It took awhile to get home from that disaster, I can tell you.

And now that you've read it, you're prepped. You understand the fundamentals and you can't wait to get started. Skip to **Scenario C**. But, if you still haven't read it…

SCENARIO B

There is still a lot we can work on. Know this: determination, hard work, and a willingness to stretch yourself are the ingredients you need to become Awesome at anything. If you believe this, then you're already on the journey. There will be mistakes along the way, but that's okay. This book is here to help you handle them.

AND FINALLY, SCENARIO C …

Great. We're all on the same page. Ready to start work on our journey to becoming Awesome? Before we begin, I want you to remember a few things:

O This book is full of fantastic tips and hints to help you think about becoming Awesome. Do some of them. Do all of them. Do one of them. It doesn't matter. Just give it a try and start somewhere. I suspect you'll surprise yourself.

O Being Awesome is about being the best you can be. If you don't even try, you'll never know just how great you could get. But it is easy to be daunted by taking on a new challenge. At the end of this, it doesn't matter if you don't become a professional athlete or the president. What matters is that you get out there, take a risk, and dare to fail.

O If you ever meet my mom, don't mention magnets.

SO, LET'S GO!

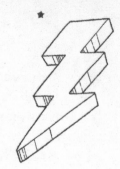

"YOUR SUCCESS
will be determined by your own
CONFIDENCE
and
FORTITUDE."

Michelle Obama

LAWYER, FORMER FIRST LADY, AND AWESOME CREW MEMBER

1.

AVERAGE OR AWESOME?

ARE YOU IN A GROWTH OR FIXED MINDSET?

Which sounds most like you?

14

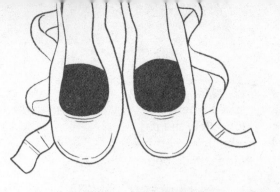

IN THEIR SHOES

Think of a successful person you really admire. It could be someone in sports, in music, on TV, an author, an actor, or even a teacher. (No, I'm not kidding. Teachers can be Awesome, right?) It might seem like they were destined for success, but put yourself in their shoes. Do some research to see what has really helped them get to the top. How have they managed to achieve their dreams?

FAMOUS PERSON:..

WHY DO YOU ADMIRE THEM?

....

....

....

....

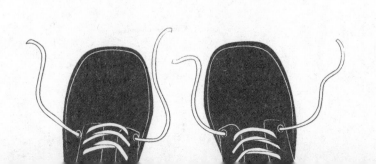

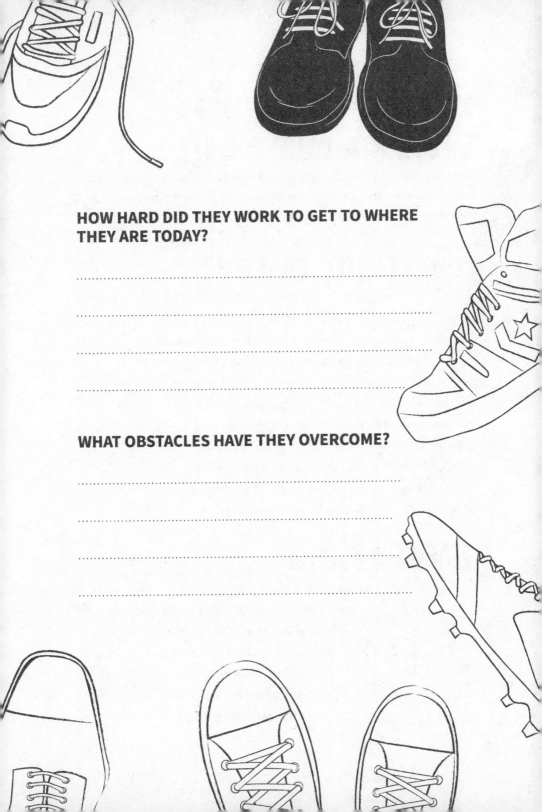

HOW HARD DID THEY WORK TO GET TO WHERE THEY ARE TODAY?

....

....

....

....

WHAT OBSTACLES HAVE THEY OVERCOME?

....

....

....

....

IF THEY CAN DO IT, WHY CAN'T YOU?

Don't forget: no one is born a superstar or a world champion. Let the legends below inspire you that no matter where you start from, with perseverance and hard work, you can end up making progress that might surprise you!

TOM DALEY

Tom Daley grew up in Plymouth, England, and was fascinated by the divers he saw at his local swimming pool. At eight years old, he joined a diving club and got to work honing his skills. But he faced a fork in the road when his tough training schedule clashed with his judo practice, which he also loved. Tom made the difficult decision to focus his hard work on diving, which paid off when he became the youngest person ever to win the British under-eighteen national junior platform title, competing against people seven years his senior. He now has **TWO** Olympic bronze medals under his belt.

ZAHA HADID

Although Zaha Hadid came from a privileged Iraqi family, she had to work exceptionally hard to succeed as both a woman and an Arab Muslim in the white male-dominated world of architecture. As a result, the profession was opened up to other women in a new way and her legacy continues to push boundaries in the field after her death.

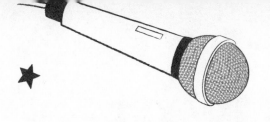

OPRAH WINFREY

Oprah Winfrey struggled in school and was bullied by her peers for being poor. But determined not to give up, she transferred schools and gained a full scholarship to Tennessee State University. It wasn't long before she attracted the attention of a local radio station and became a part-time newscaster. She spent years practicing on TV and radio shows, but it all paid off when she was given *The Oprah Winfrey Show.*

ROALD DAHL

Roald Dahl was born in the UK to Norwegian parents. His father and sister died when he was very young, and he was sent to boarding school, which he hated. Many of the teachers there inspired the villains in his children's books. Thought to have been dyslexic, Roald was never regarded as particularly talented at school, especially at writing. While serving as a pilot in the Second World War, he was seriously injured in a plane crash. In spite of his difficulties, Roald poured his life experiences into his writing, and went on to become one of the most beloved children's authors of all time.

LET'S GET TO YET

Sometimes the way we think about our abilities can limit us. Stop us from even trying. But we know we can become Awesome if we are in the right mindset and are willing to put in the effort. So, make the word YET your new BFF. And when you think "I can't do it," add your new best friend and say "I can't do it YET" instead. It will help you see your challenge as a journey and help you think about the steps you need to take to tackle it.

EMBRACE THE POWER OF... YET!

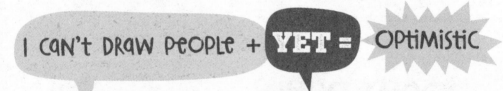

I can't draw people + YET = Optimistic

This equation isn't right + YET = EMPOWERING

I can't play the trumpet + YET = Growth Mindset

"I keep on making what I can't do yet in order to learn to be able to do it."
VINCENT VAN GOGH, AWESOME PAINTER

20

LIST SOME OF THE THINGS YOU CAN'T DO ... YET!

(I've added one of my own to get you started ...)

I CAN'T COOK. *(Seriously, it is an issue. Last week I actually burned some breakfast cereal. I'd heard that warm milk was nice on cornflakes. No one mentioned that you shouldn't heat the milk and flakes together!) But I have decided that* I CAN'T COOK YET *and am going to buy a simple cookbook. I won't be Gordon Ramsay anytime soon, but I'll be able to boil an egg.*

...YET!

...YET!

...YET!

FORK IN THE ROAD

First things first: no, I don't mean **THAT** kind of fork. **THAT** kind of fork is great for eating your dad's french fries when he isn't looking, but much less useful for finding out about the kinds of challenges that people have met in their lives!

A fork in the road is a **METAPHOR** for moments in life when perhaps a **BIG** choice comes along and you have to decide which "path" to take.

You may not have faced these types of decisions yet, but it's highly likely that your parents or other adults in your life have.

Talk to them about when they faced their own "fork in the road" and what they decided to do. Scribble down your findings on the next page…

1 WHO DID I TALK TO?

....

....

....

....

....

....

2 WHAT CHOICE DID THEY FACE?

....

....

....

....

....

....

3 WHAT DID THEY DECIDE TO DO?

....

....

....

....

....

4 WOULD THEY DO ANYTHING DIFFERENTLY NOW?

....

....

....

....

STEP AWAY FROM THE COMFORT ZONE

You're probably thinking that your comfort zone is your nice cozy bedroom or the sofa where you beat your best friend at video games. Well, yes, those places are comfortable, but your "comfort zone" is not a physical place—it's a space in your head where you feel safe, and that doesn't stretch you beyond what you **THINK** you can do.

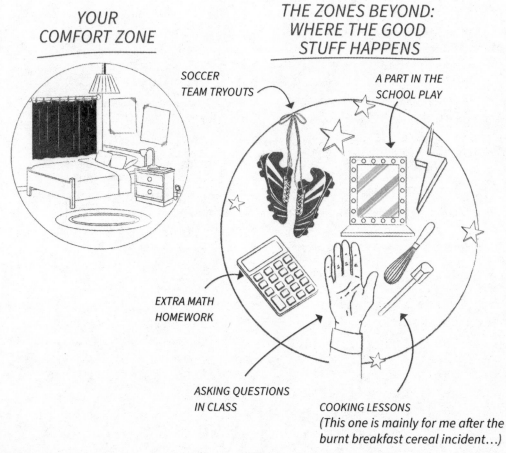

YOUR COMFORT ZONE

THE ZONES BEYOND: WHERE THE GOOD STUFF HAPPENS

SOCCER TEAM TRYOUTS

A PART IN THE SCHOOL PLAY

EXTRA MATH HOMEWORK

ASKING QUESTIONS IN CLASS

COOKING LESSONS (This one is mainly for me after the burnt breakfast cereal incident…)

Can you see? Pushing yourself out of your comfort zone (i.e., your bedroom!) means saying **YES** to things and doing activities that you might not ordinarily do, perhaps because they challenge you or might even scare you a little bit. Now complete this diagram to show activities that you consider to be:

Comfort zone   *Stretching myself zone*

Things-that-maybe-freak-me-out-but-I'm-still-going-to-try zone

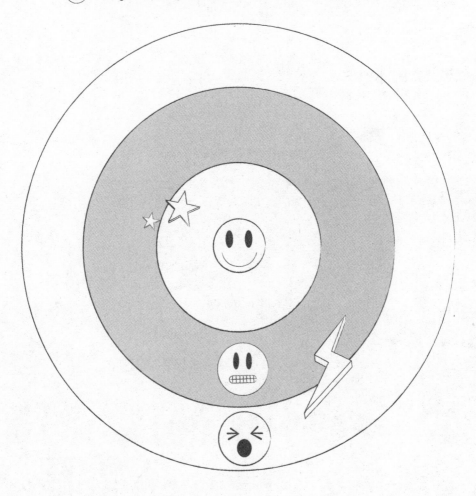

SUCCESS IS LIKE AN ICEBERG

When you only see somebody's performance, you don't see all the determination, hard work, and effort that has gone into it. It's a bit like looking at the tip of an iceberg.

WHAT PEOPLE SEE

SUCCESS!

WHAT PEOPLE DON'T SEE

DeDiCation

Persistence

DISCIPLINE

Disappointment

FAILURE

HARD WORK

SaCRifiCe

What will you have to do to achieve your goal?

MY GOAL

·· ·· · · · ·· · · ·· · · ·· ·

**WHAT I'LL DO
TO ACHIEVE IT**

· ·

· ·

· ·

· ·

Based on drawing by @sylviaduckworth

"It's not that I'm **SO SMART,** it's just that **I STAY** with **PROBLEMS** longer."

Albert Einstein

AWESOME SCIENTIST WITH A GROWTH MINDSET

28

HOW CONFIDENT DO YOU FEEL YOU ARE?

I once went to a party. I was so nervous about "having to dance" that I actually hid behind the curtain in the local church hall. My friend Mark, on the other hand, had no such concerns—I had never seen anything like it, until I saw Beyoncé several years later. As we left, I felt totally deflated. He'd had the best time while my confidence had held me back, and I'd spent the whole night looking at the inside of a window curtain.

So, how confident do you feel you are?

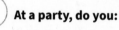

1 **At a party, do you:**
- **A.** Walk up to the nearest person and start talking.
- **B.** Take a deep breath and look for someone you know.
- **C.** If there's no one you know, call your parents and beg for a lift home.
- **D.** Only go to a party if you can arrive with a friend.

2 **Do you feel like your opinion matters?**
- **A.** Yes.
- **B.** Yes, but not everyone thinks so.
- **C.** No one cares.
- **D.** I don't have opinions.

3 **If you try something new and it doesn't go as planned, do you think:**
- **A.** That's okay, I'll work on nailing it next time.
- **B.** Shrug, it went well enough.

C. Same old, same old. I'm hopeless.

D. Never doing that again.

 When you've achieved something, do you think:

A. I knew if I worked hard enough, I could do it.

B. It was touch and go, but I thought I could probably do it.

C. I bet everyone has done way better.

D. I just got lucky.

 If you spot a nightmare homework question, do you:

A. Take it on, think about your practice, and really try to figure it out. You know help is out there, but you want to have a go first.

B. Make a quick start and then ask for help.

C. Start and then give up.

D. Don't even finish reading it through.

 If your best friend does something that upsets you, can you talk to them about how you feel?

A. Always.

B. Most of the time.

C. Sometimes.

D. Never.

 When you're out and about, how do you feel about talking to new people?

A. No problem—I love making new friends.

B. Okay, but it can be a little scary if I don't know anyone.

C. Really hate it—I'd much prefer to stick to my existing friends.

D. I'd avoid it like the plague.

WHAT YOUR ANSWERS MEAN

First, score your answers.

A = 4 points
B = 3 points
C = 2 points
D = 1 point

IF YOU SCORED BETWEEN 20 AND 28 POINTS

You're generally pretty confident and you're not especially scared of mistakes, which helps you learn from experience. Warning alert: sometimes being overconfident can stop you from stretching and challenging yourself.

IF YOU SCORED BETWEEN 12 AND 19 POINTS

If you don't face anything too challenging that day, your confidence is okay. But other times, you're having to fake it a bit to get through. Remind yourself about all the things you have successfully achieved to improve your resilience.

IF YOU SCORED BETWEEN 7 AND 11 POINTS

You're probably putting yourself down a bit, believing that there's no way you can achieve things you actually **CAN** do. This fixed mindset could really be holding you back, so don't forget to challenge your negative thoughts and push yourself outside of your comfort zone from time to time.

"If my **MIND** can conceive it, and my **HEART** can **BELIEVE IT,** I know I can **ACHIEVE IT."**

Jesse Jackson
AWESOME CIVIL RIGHTS ACTIVIST

DON'T HOLD BACK

Now, be totally honest with yourself and really think about which negative thoughts race through your mind and hold you back from achieving your dreams. Write them down in the thought bubbles—I've suggested a couple of common thoughts to get you going …

I'M SO MUCH WORSE than EVERYONE ELSE at SOCCER.

35

DUMP YOUR NEGATIVE THOUGHTS

Well done, you've brain-dumped your negative thoughts on the previous pages. It's these fixed mindset thoughts that will stop you from being the very best you can be. So let's figure out how you can turn those negatives on their head and make them much more positive.

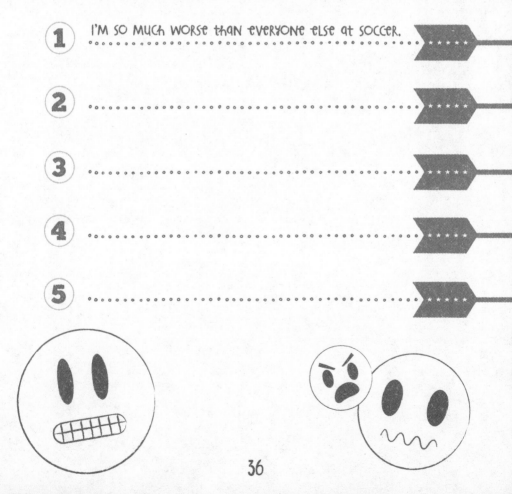

1 I'M SO MUCH WORSE than EVERYONE ELSE at SOCCER.

2

3

4

5

I CAN GET BETTER AT SOCCER BY PRACTICING WITH MY SISTER. SHE'S OLDER AND BETTER, AND WILL HELP ME IMPROVE.

....

....

....

....

....

"There will be
OBSTACLES.
There will be
DOUBTERS.
There will be
MISTAKES.
But with
HARD WORK...
there are
NO LIMITS."

Michael Phelps
MOST DECORATED OLYMPIAN OF ALL TIME

So, without those negative thoughts holding you back, it's time to put on your success goggles. This is your chance to

THINK BIG! What are your **NO LIMITS**

dreams? Get your dreaming cap on and list them here…

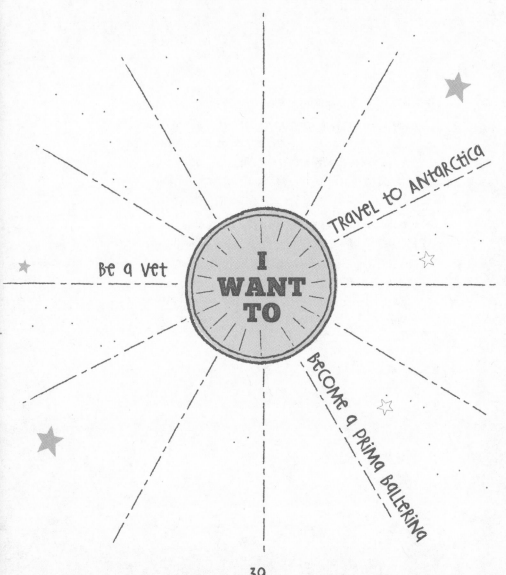

Travel to Antarctica

Be a vet

I WANT TO

Become a prima ballerina

39

AFRAID TO FAIL?

What would you do in your day-to-day life if you weren't afraid of failing, or looking stupid in front of your friends? List some things here (I've made some suggestions of my own to get you started …).

○ **Sing in a band.** *I've always (silently) rated my singing voice. I like to think—only to myself—that if One Direction ever re-form, then I could replace Zayn. But the truth is, I have never actually sung a note in public and I am a bit frightened that everyone would think I was terrible.*

○ **Cook dinner for my family.** *My brother hasn't enjoyed anything other than a frozen meal since the invention of the microwave. I know my parents would love it, but I fear the humiliation when my burgers are raw and my french fries are charcoal.*

Your turn…

○

○

Now I'd like to see you **REALLY** push yourself out of your comfort zone—try out one or two of the things on your list (nothing dangerous please, definitely no throwing of magnets) and write those in the box below.

WHAT DID YOU TRY?

WHAT HAPPENED?

WHAT ARE YOU GOING TO TRY NEXT?

MY ~~MISTAKS~~ MISTAKES DIARY

Mistakes are great. Yes, really great. They help us to understand what we don't know so that we can decide how we fix the gaps in our knowledge or skills.

I MAKE TONS OF MISTAKES.

Getting on a bus to the wrong country, for example, that was a big one. (You'll need to read *You Are Awesome* for the full story.) At school, I never seemed to have the right stuff in my bag. Everyone else seemed to manage to have the right books, the right homework, and the right PE clothes. Not me. I'd arrive without the physics homework, but carrying the 3D model of the Empire State Building I'd made for the history project, which wasn't needed for three more days. And then getting the right stuff home again was an even bigger problem. I once came back wearing only one shoe! How does that even happen?

How we recover from our mistakes is crucial. We can choose to hide away, pretend the whole event never happened, and vow to never try again. Or, we can seize the opportunity to consider what we might do differently next time.

"COULDN'T YOU tell that you were WALKING in a SOCK?"

Keeping a mistakes diary helps you to see the patterns in your behavior that may be causing the problem. Here's one of my mistake-diary pages to give you an idea of how it works.

MONDAY

MISTAKE I MADE

Coming home with only one shoe.

WHY DID I MAKE IT?

Getting changed in a rush after PE.

WHAT CAN I LEARN FROM IT?

Allow more time after PE so I'm not rushing as much...and always check my feet!

Try recording some of your own mistakes here.

MONDAY

MISTAKE I MADE

WHY DID I MAKE IT?

WHAT CAN I LEARN FROM IT?

TUESDAY

MISTAKE I MADE

Got 7 out of 10 on the spelling test.

WHY DID I MAKE IT?

Too confident. Thought I knew them and so I didn't practice.

WHAT CAN I LEARN FROM IT?

Don't assume I'm already great. I need to put in some extra effort next week.

WEDNESDAY

MISTAKE I MADE

WHY DID I MAKE IT?

WHAT CAN I LEARN FROM IT?

THURSDAY

MISTAKE I MADE

WHY DID I MAKE IT?

WHAT CAN I LEARN FROM IT?

FRIDAY

MISTAKE I MADE

WHY DID I MAKE IT?

WHAT CAN I LEARN FROM IT?

SATURDAY

MISTAKE I MADE

WHY DID I MAKE IT?

WHAT CAN I LEARN FROM IT?

SUNDAY

MISTAKE I MADE

Shouted at my mom on the way back from a hockey match.

WHY DID I MAKE IT?

I was frustrated that we'd lost. I took it out on her.

WHAT CAN I LEARN FROM IT?

She sacrificed her time to take me. I should be more considerate.

DO YOU FIND YOURSELF MAKING the SAME KIND OF MISTAKES OVER AND OVER AGAIN?

"I BELIEVE
that one of life's
GREATEST
RISKS
is never DARING
TO RISK."

Oprah Winfrey
ENTREPRENEUR, DOER OF GOOD DEEDS, AND AWESOME TV STAR

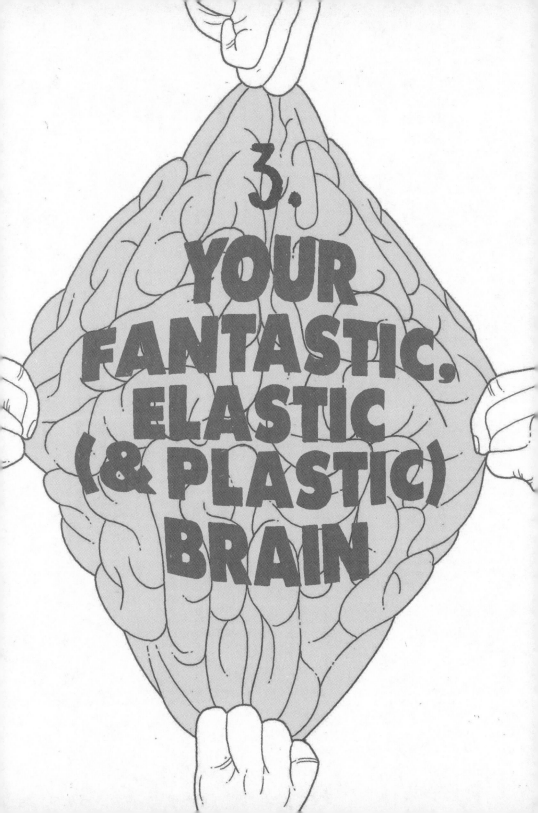

3.

YOUR FANTASTIC, ELASTIC (& PLASTIC) BRAIN

TRUTH OR BUSTED?

Your brain is your biggest ally on your mission to be Awesome. It's the most powerful machine in the universe! But which of the facts below are **TRUE** or **FALSE**?

1.
Your brain is composed of more than 70 PERCENT water.

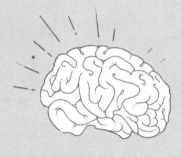

2.
There are around 100,000 Miles of BLOOD vessels in the human Brain.

3.
Your brain has the capacity to POWER a SMALL LIGHTBULB.

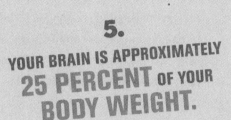

4.
YOU ONLY USE
10 PERCENT
OF YOUR BRAIN.

5.
YOUR BRAIN IS APPROXIMATELY
25 PERCENT OF YOUR
BODY WEIGHT.

6.
You can't
TICKLE
YOURSELF
because your
brain prevents it.

7.
NEURONS send
information to your
brain at 62 mph!

TRAIN YOUR BRAIN

Your brain is amazing. Did you know that it actually grows when you do things that you find challenging? It's true! When we stretch ourselves by coming out of our comfort zone, we create new connections in our brains. These become stronger the more we practice and—here's the bad news—the **MORE DIFFICULT** the practice is too.

So, let's think about what "hard practice" looks like:

GROW-YOUR-BRAIN PRACTICE

○ Those tricky math problems I've been putting off.

○ ....

....

○ ....

....

○ ....

....

MIGHT-NOT-GROW-YOUR-BRAIN PRACTICE

○ Practicing the easy questions from my favorite math topic—the ones I know I can definitely get right.

○ ....

....

○ ....

....

○ ....

....

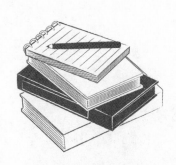

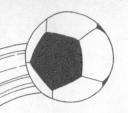

USE IT OR LOSE IT

Some even worse news: if you stop practicing, those brain connections can start to fade away! Now, I don't practice my chop loop every day (that's a seriously hard table-tennis shot, in case you were wondering), and as a result I'm just not as good at it anymore.

Think about something you used to be good at but have now gotten out of the habit of doing. Some examples could be…

○ **Playing the piano**

○ **Speaking French**

○ ....

○ ....

○ ....

○ ....

○ ....

○ ....

PARLEZ-VOUS FRANÇAIS?

OVER THE SCHOOL BREAK, I FORGOT HOW TO ...

○ ....

○ ....

○ ....

○ ....

○ ....

○ ....

FREE UP YOUR BRAIN!

Do you know what your "working" memory is? Well, it's the ability you have to instantly process new information. To (for example) listen to a set of instructions and follow them, or to do a bit of mental arithmetic in your head.

But guess what? Our working memory has a bit of a limit on it. We can't follow the instructions if there are too many of them. And we can find it difficult to do two things at once. My mom can't text and walk at the same time, for example.

TRY TAPPING YOUR HEAD and RUBBING YOUR TUMMY at the same time... NOt easy!

I'm getting to the point, I promise. When we are learning new things, it makes sense to be focused and ensure that we are not using up our limited capacity with pointless distractions. If you're looking at a picture of Noah Centineo at the same time as doing your math homework, that is likely to cause a distraction. So, put it away (no, not the math homework, the picture of Noah Centineo!) because Noah is taking up some valuable bit of your processing capacity, meaning you won't have all the room you need in your brain for the tricky sums. Worries and concerns can also take up brain space and cause us to lose focus.

Try some of the following to free up your brain and let it focus on what really matters!

○ **If you're trying to remember something for later, write it down!** By making a to-do list, you no longer take up space in your brain desperately trying to remember all the things you need to do. Simple!

○ **Try out the Worry Jar exercise on page 112**—sometimes writing down your anxieties can mean you focus less on them.

○ **Avoid multitasking!** By trying to do too many things at once, you'll fill your brain up with unnecessary detail. So, forget trying to do your math homework while attempting a Rachael Ray–style version of mac and cheese.

○ **Avoid listening to loud music with lyrics.** Your poor old brain will have to work harder while it processes the words going into your ears!

○ **Make up with your pesky brother.** He might be **THE MOST ANNOYING** kid in the world, but thinking about ways to exact a super revenge can take up space in your brain that you could use for practicing that class presentation.

Focus

FORGET ME NOT

Life is busy, right? There's so much going on, what with school, friends, family stuff, hobbies, keeping up with the latest shows, games, social media. Phew. No wonder we sometimes forget things! We tend to live our lives in the **NOW**, always moving forward and trying to understand and respond to things as we go. So is it any wonder that we forget the Spanish vocab that we learned so well just a week ago?

The graph (this is actual science, you know) on the opposite page shows how information is gradually lost from your memory if you only absorb it once. But the more times you go over it, the more of it you remember. It explains why studying is so important—and why refreshing your memory on each topic throughout the year will be **WAY** more helpful than cramming the night before the exam.

So the moral of this story is that if you want to learn something and retain it, you need to practice it regularly, as you will have a much greater chance of retaining it! And don't beat yourself up if you can't do something the first time around…or even the second time. Just keep going!

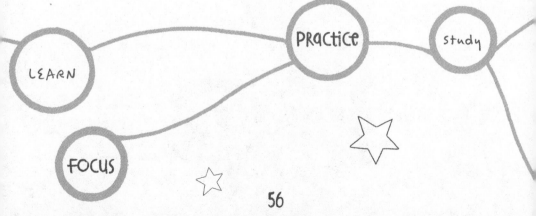

LEARN

FOCUS

PRACTICE

study

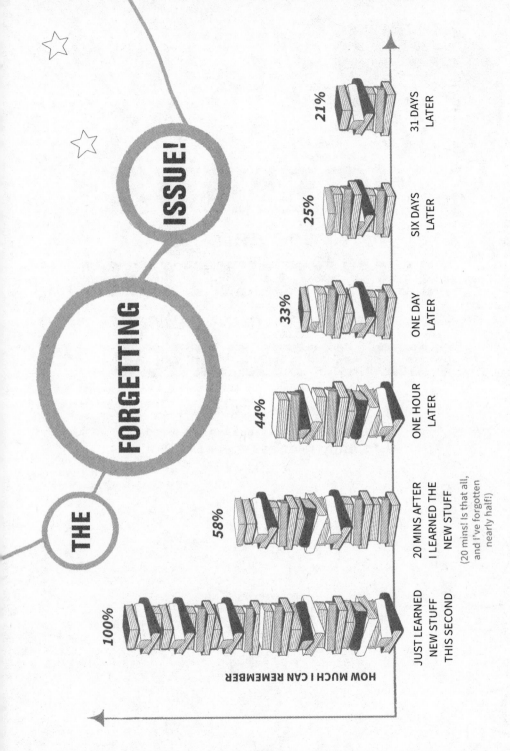

THE

FORGETTING

ISSUE!

HOW MUCH I CAN REMEMBER

100%
JUST LEARNED NEW STUFF THIS SECOND

58%
20 MINS AFTER I LEARNED THE NEW STUFF
(20 mins! Is that all, and I've forgotten nearly half!)

44%
ONE HOUR LATER

33%
ONE DAY LATER

25%
SIX DAYS LATER

21%
31 DAYS LATER

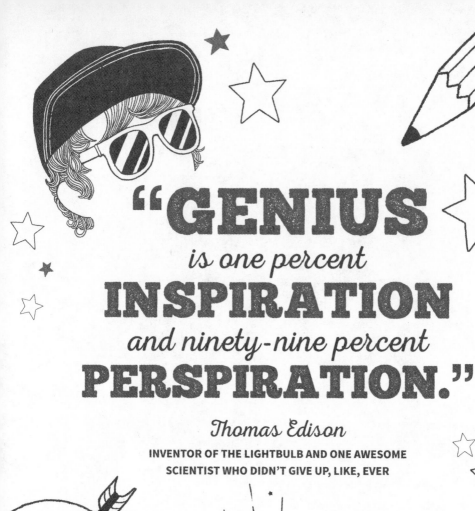

"GENIUS
is one percent
INSPIRATION
and ninety-nine percent
PERSPIRATION."

Thomas Edison

**INVENTOR OF THE LIGHTBULB AND ONE AWESOME
SCIENTIST WHO DIDN'T GIVE UP, LIKE, EVER**

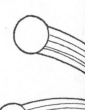

4.

PRACTICE MAKES ~~PERFECT~~ AWESOME

THE BEST YOU CAN BE?

It's great to feel like you're the best at something, but…
how do you know you're the best you can be?

Time to get really honest with yourself. What's something you feel confident about being good at?

. . . .

Are you pushing yourself as hard as you could be?

A Yes, I'm trying my absolute best.

B I'm working hard but could be doing more.

C I'm doing okay.

D If I'm honest, I mostly do this on autopilot.

E
OKay, I aDMit it. I WORK at the PACE of a TORTOISE.

60

If you didn't choose , what are you going to do to keep challenging yourself?

S-T-R-E-T-C-H Y-O-U-R-S-E-L-F

We all like to stretch. My dad likes to stretch a little too much. He used to do lunges in the kitchen at breakfast time. In Lycra and a sports headband. Quite possibly that might be what has put me off cooking. This isn't the sort of stretching I'm talking about. I'm talking about the type of practice that really pushes you to be the best you can be, whether you want to be a hotshot at tennis, a physicist to rival Stephen Hawking, or the best speaker your debate club has ever had!

DIARY OF AN AWESOME PUBLIC SPEAKER
Monday, February 27

*I gave a presentation today and didn't feel I performed at my best. So tonight I practiced in front of the mirror (and my dog) to try and get more confident. The dog clearly reckons that this is my **Basic Practice**, so I'll have to push myself out of my comfort zone if I want to really improve.*

WEDNESDAY, MARCH 15

*For my **Advanced Practice**, I'm going to write some of my own speeches and discuss them with the head of my debate club, getting ideas for how to make them better.*

SATURDAY, SEPTEMBER 8

*Today I plucked up the courage to actually participate in a session at the debate club, where they throw out a topic and you have to instantly get to your feet and speak to a room of twenty people about it. It's pretty nerve-racking, but this **Be My Best Practice** will really push me to my limits! I'm going to keep attending the debate club every other week for as long as it takes for me to really nail public speaking.*

Now, think about your goal and what you can do to stretch yourself toward achieving it. Set some challenging practices that will push you out of your comfort zone.

○ ....

○ ....

○ ....

○ ....

○ ....

○ ....

○ ....

○ ....

GETTING DOWN TO BUSINESS

So, we've got your practice nailed. Let's focus on, um…your **FOCUS**.

1 PRACTICE SPACE

Make sure the environment is right. If you're learning Russian, all you may need is a quiet area, but if you're determined to master skateboard tricks, you'll need S P A C E !

2 EQUIPMENT

Make sure you have all the equipment and gear you need on hand. So for learning Russian, you might need a notebook, a pen, a desk lamp, and a voice recorder, for example. For skateboarding tricks, make sure you have a skateboard (duh), kneepads, and a helmet (and possibly a few bandages!).

3 TIDY UP

If you are working at a desk studying or learning, **TIDY IT UP**. This sounds like a silly one, but believe me, it helps 100 percent with your focus, as you will no longer be stressing about finding that bit of paper with the special Russian vocab on it. My mom always used to tell me that mess causes stress. I didn't believe her at the time, but now I totally get it…

4 DISTRACTIONS

Remove distractions such as little sisters, and turn off or silence your smartphones so you won't be troubled by the pings, blips, and beeps of your emails and alerts coming in.

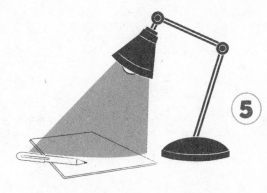

5 MAKE IT PUBLIC

Announce your goal to the world and let everyone know what you are aiming to do. By "going public" with your goal, it will be more **REAL** and will give you the motivation to achieve it. The people around you will also check in with you on your goal, giving you an even greater boost to succeed!

6 FOOD & DRINK

Keep food and drinks on hand for sustenance, energy, and to keep hydrated. But also to avoid the temptation of disappearing off to find snacks …

PACKING IT ALL IN

So you've got a plan for some goals and you know you're going to have to practice if you're going to achieve them. Nailing them is going to take up quite a lot of time, and let's

	MORNING	*AFTERNOON*
MON		
TUES		
WED		
THURS		
FRI		
SAT		
SUN		

face it, you probably don't have lots of spare time to begin with. So let's try and figure out how you can possibly fit it all in. Use a pencil (keep an eraser nearby!) to map out what you're trying to fit into your week. When you're at school, what opportunities in classes or clubs might you have to work on your goals?

EVENING	TO RELAX, I WILL

MAKING FRIENDS WITH FEEDBACK

Listening to constructive feedback is an essential part of improving at anything. But do you take feedback well, or do you get defensive as soon as anyone suggests ways you could do better? I suggested once that my brother change his table-tennis serve to get a bit more spin. I thought I was helping but he definitely did not. He wouldn't practice with me for two weeks after that.

I have a **DEEP SUSPICION** that my **"LUCKY"** table-tennis ball didn't get taken by a **FOX** one night as he still claims to this day.

So, take this quiz to find out just how you feel about feedback!

1 **You receive a bad grade on a test you thought you did really well on. Do you:**

A. Protest against the grade. What you wrote was brilliant!

B. Walk home feeling miserable. You're such a failure.

C. Go to the extra tutoring sessions your teacher suggests. You know it will help you for the next test.

2 Your best friend is annoyed because you're always late when you hang out. Do you:

A. Start listing all of the things they've done wrong lately.

B. Tell them you can't help it—it just happens!

C. Apologize and promise to make it next time.

3 Your mom suggests that you could do more to help out around the house. Do you:

A. Tell her you already help out a lot. You made your bed last week (or was it the week before that?).

B. Say you would help, but you're useless at cleaning—she'd just end up doing it all again.

C. Ask her what else you could be doing to help out.

4 Your basketball coach tells you that you need to work on your technique if you want to score more points. What do you do?

A. Change nothing. If she didn't think you were any good, she wouldn't have put you on the team.

B. Tell her you'll never be as good as some of the other players—they're just more nimble than you are.

C. Ask the coach for some pointers—she definitely knows what she's talking about.

69

Time to see if there are any patterns in your answers.

If you chose:

MOSTLY A

Whoa, hold up there! You brush off any negative feedback and are convinced that feedback isn't something you'll benefit from. You might not like hearing criticism, but try to see it as a way to help you improve.

MOSTLY B

Ouch, you take feedback to heart. But when people offer you suggestions for improvement, they're not saying you're a failure. Find your confidence and believe that if you work hard, it will pay off.

MOSTLY C

You're Awesome at accepting feedback! You're always happy to hear how you can improve and do better. Not only do you listen, but you act on it too.

Take feedback on board!

"You might never fail on the scale I did, but some **FAILURE** in life is **INEVITABLE.** It is impossible to live **WITHOUT FAILING** at something, unless you live so **CAUTIOUSLY** that you might as well **NOT HAVE LIVED AT ALL—** in which case, **YOU FAIL** by **DEFAULT."**

J.K. Rowling

HARRY POTTER CREATOR, MISTAKE-MAKER EXTRAORDINAIRE, AND AWESOME HUMAN BEING

MY FEEDBACK SQUAD

Everyone needs a feedback squad. My mom, my coach, and my friend Mark were definitely in mine. Always prepared to give me their honest opinion. In fact, so was my brother. And although he was always more than willing to tell me exactly where I was going wrong, he was usually right (never tell him that ...).

Which questions would you ask a feedback squad?

? . . . .

? . . . .

? . . . .

? . . . .

? . . . .

? . . . .

In the space below, draw the people who are prepared to give you honest feedback. Is it a parent, caregiver, sister, brother (you're kidding, right?), friend, favorite aunt/uncle, teacher, coach, your local grocer, or librarian? (Okay, this is getting silly now.)

"You're **NOT** meant to **DO WHAT'S EASY.** You're meant to **CHALLENGE YOURSELF."**

Justin Timberlake
SINGER-SONGWRITER AND AWESOME COMEBACK KID

74

5.

SMASHING THE MYTHS OF SUCCESS

SOME OF MY GROWTH MINDSET HEROES

There are so many well-known people out there who achieved things against the odds. Here are just two of my favorite stories—but why don't you try to find some yourself? You could build yourself a Mindset Heroes portfolio!

MARTA VIEIRA DA SILVA

Brazilian soccer star Marta grew up in a poor family. She began playing street soccer in her local neighborhood, but she was often shunned by the boys, who didn't like the fact that a girl could outplay them. She managed to persuade her brothers to let her attend their training sessions, and once selected to their team, the brilliant young striker was never overlooked again. Marta left home at the age of fourteen, taking an arduous three-day bus trip to the city of Rio de Janeiro, to join her first professional soccer team, Vasco da Gama. Marta was voted the FIFA Women's World Player of the Year for five consecutive years from 2006 to 2010 and today is considered a legend of the game.

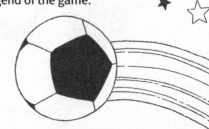

ABRAHAM LINCOLN

Abraham Lincoln was one of the greatest presidents in U.S. history, but it is said that he lacked a formal education and the usual leadership qualities of charm, charisma, and friends in high places. Abraham was born in a one-room cabin in Kentucky to uneducated parents who farmed for a living. Abraham largely taught himself; he was an avid reader and consumed vast quantities of books on every topic. At the age of twenty-two, he set off in his canoe all on his own with only a few belongings to his name. He took on the enormous task of teaching himself the law and became a successful lawyer. When he lost his campaign for the U.S. Senate in 1858, he was not deterred. Abraham showed his resilience and eventually won the U.S. presidency in 1860.

DIY (DESIGN IT YOURSELF)

It can be really useful to stick a poster of your biggest achievements or favorite quotes on your bedroom wall to keep you motivated. Try designing your own mindset poster here— what would you choose to include? What does growth mindset mean to YOU?

Once you've got your design, get to work on the real poster using a massive piece of paper!

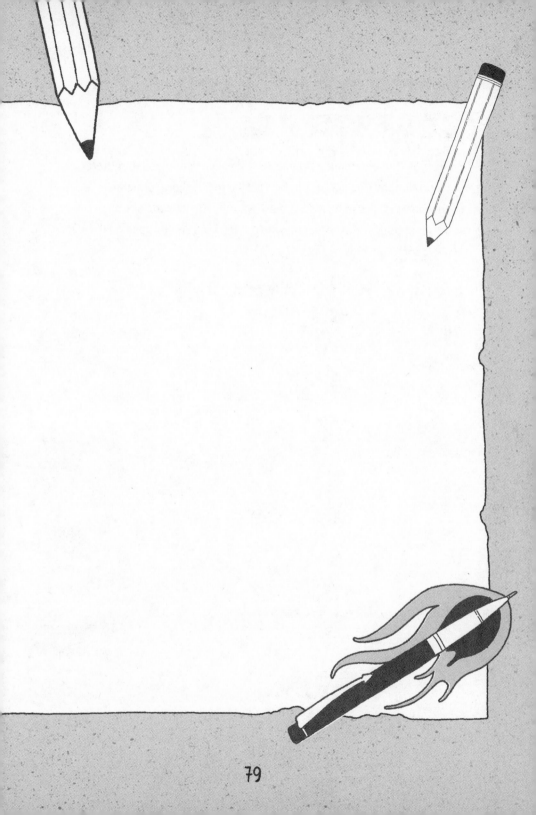

YOUR REAL-LIFE SUPERHEROES

Earlier you thought about a celebrity who really inspires you. But there are lots of impressive people in your real life too. Is there someone in class who you'd like to be like? Is there a family friend who has done some great things? Has someone who has left your school gone on to achieve something Awesome?

I want to be better at...

1 Math

2

3

4

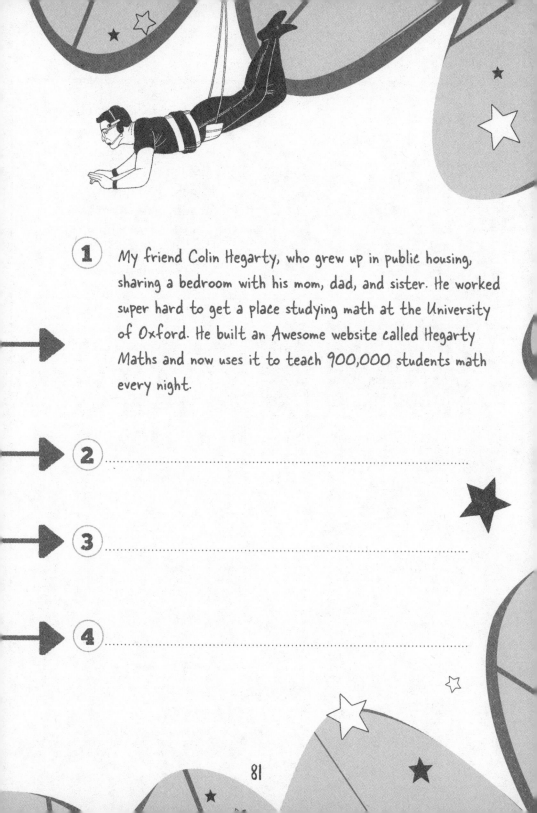

1 My friend Colin Hegarty, who grew up in public housing, sharing a bedroom with his mom, dad, and sister. He worked super hard to get a place studying math at the University of Oxford. He built an Awesome website called Hegarty Maths and now uses it to teach 900,000 students math every night.

2 ....

3 ....

4 ....

GET THE SCOOP

All the people you listed on the previous pages are bound to have great stories to tell about how they got so good. Ask as many of them as possible the following questions and note down their answers.

HOW GOOD
WERE YOU WHEN YOU FIRST STARTED?

WHAT
SETBACKS
DID YOU FACE?

HOW DID YOU OVERCOME THEM?

WHAT'S YOUR TOP PIECE OF ADVICE FOR ME?

TURNING POINTS

Sometimes it's easy to think that world champions and superstars were always destined to get to the top. But often, it all started for them when they had the guts to grab an opportunity.
Did you know...

When **TAYLOR SWIFT** was twelve, her computer broke and a repairman came over to fix it. He picked up an old guitar lying around the Swift house and started playing. She asked him to teach her how to play, which jump-started her passion for songwriting and got her practicing for hours.

In the early years of his career, **MARK HAMILL** was shuffling between small parts on TV shows and films until he landed a lead role in a new family drama. It could have been his big break, but just before production started on the show, he found out he'd been cast as Luke Skywalker in *Star Wars*. Taking a huge risk, Hamill decided to drop the TV show and go for the movie instead—and the rest is history.

Shawn Corey Carter, later known as **JAY-Z**, grew up in a housing project in Brooklyn with three siblings raised by a single mom. He was always banging out drum patterns on the kitchen table and writing lyrics, but he couldn't get a major label to sign him. He didn't give up though.

He sold his own CDs out of his car until he eventually helped found an independent record label that released his debut album. It was so successful that he's gone on to release twelve more albums, sell over 100 million records worldwide, establish successful clothing and restaurant businesses, and, of course, marry Beyoncé.

Taylor, Mark, and JAY-Z all seized opportunities when they came knocking. So think about it. If you took advantage of something unexpected, what might happen for you?

1 . . . .

2 . . . .

3 . . . .

4 . . . .

5 . . . .

PASSING IT ON

A growth mindset isn't all about helping yourself. It can also make you an expert advisor when it comes to your friends. Try this quiz to see if you're helping your friends toward a growth mindset.

 Sasha is devastated when she learns she hasn't made the soccer team. Do you say:

A. Your ball skills are amazing; the coach must be nuts. You don't want to play for a team that doesn't realize what an asset you'd be.

B. What did you find the trickiest in the tryouts? Let's practice that and get prepared for the tryout next term.

Sajid is fed up—his brother Muhammad is ALWAYS better than him at everything, and to top it all off, Muhammad has just won a scholarship to a fancy school. Sajid says he's never going to be able to match up. Do you say:

A. Muhammad is a loser; all he does is study. Why would you want to be like him?

B. I bet the competition between you and Muhammad pushes both of you to be better. Why don't you ask him to give you some feedback on your English essay?

 Luke has a big violin performance coming up in a few days. He's been practicing really hard, but the thought of all the people in the audience is making him sick with nerves.

Do you say:

A. You've been working so hard—that's the important thing, not the performance itself. Why don't you skip it if you don't feel up to it that night?

B. Performing is so nerve-racking, but getting other people to listen to you is part of what makes playing so great. Just think of how you'll feel when you do nail it—and how much easier it'll feel the next time around.

4 Layla has a big science project next due week, but she hasn't even started yet, and the panic is starting to set in. Do you say:

A. Don't worry, everyone knows you're always most efficient when you're cramming. We'll get together in a few days and do it then.

B. If you start now and stay focused, you'll be amazed at what you can do. Break it down into chunks and tackle one chunk each day.

IF YOU CHOSE MOSTLY A

You might be saying things your friends want to hear, but you're not helping them achieve a growth mindset.

IF YOU CHOSE MOSTLY B

Well done! Your encouragement is bound to keep your friends motivated and improving.

THINK OUTSIDE THE BOX

What's the one question that you get asked by adults the first time they meet you? I bet it's "What do you want to be when you get older?" You might know the answer already, which is great. But you might not have a clue and blurt out "teacher!" or "pop star!" because these are the only jobs you've heard of.

But did you know there are ALL SORTS OF JOBS out there that you've probably NEVER HEARD OF?

data detective

sloth nanny

NUCLEAR MEDICINE TECHNOLOGIST

PYTHON ENGINEER

(Don't worry if you're afraid of snakes. No slithering biters in sight.)

SPACE PSYCHOLOGIST

ANIMAL TALENT AGENT

So now that you know just how many jobs are out there, what career would you love to do?

. . . .

. . . .

. . . .

. . . .

What skills might you need to get there?

. . . .

. . . .

. . . .

. . . .

THE PODIUM OF SUCCESS

By now, you know it takes way more than a good set of genes to make it to the top. Draw yourself on the top of the podium, and then fill in some of the things you know you'll need to get there. The first three have been filled in for you...

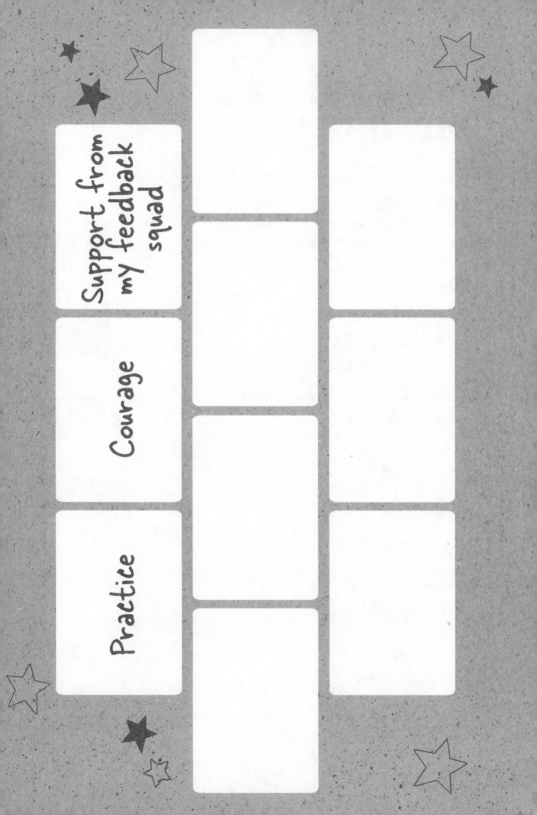

Support from my feedback squad

Courage

Practice

PLAN FOR THE DIFFICULT

It's not all going to be smooth sailing to reach your goal. So, let's anticipate as many obstacles as possible now and make a plan for overcoming them. I've added an example based on me getting better at **swimming underwater**.

GOAL:

OBSTACLE

I'm not a very quick swimmer, so I run out of breath too soon.

HOW CAN I GET AROUND IT?

Practice swimming at the surface first, to improve my stroke and get faster.

IS THIS WITHIN MY CONTROL OR OUTSIDE IT?

Within it! I can practice my stroke each time I get in the pool.

AWESOME CREW

I'll let you in on a secret. No one—and I mean no one—becomes a world champion or a business leader or a famous fashion designer all on their own. So here, think about the people in your life who can help you achieve your goals. This is your **Awesome Crew**—people who can support you, give you advice, and cheer you up when things go awry.

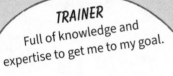

TRAINER
Full of knowledge and expertise to get me to my goal.

INSPIRATIONAL IDOL
Gives me advice based on their incredible experience.

FIXER
Troubleshoots with me when I hit an obstacle.

RAY OF SUNSHINE
Cheers me up when things don't go my way.

Here are some prompts to think about the different ways the people in our lives help us get to where we want to be. You don't have to fill in every box—start with one person you know will support you and build your crew from there.

CHEERLEADER
Believes in me and is always there cheering me on.

TRAINING BUDDY
Learns by my side and offers me tips and support.

LOGISTICS EXPERT
Brilliant at giving me lifts to practice and helping me make sure I have the right gear.

ULTIMATE RIVAL
Brings out my competitive streak and pushes me harder.

GET LYRICAL

Write down some of your favorite lyrics from songs that keep you in a growth mindset. They'll be perfect to keep you motivated when the going gets tough!

"The secret of
GETTING AHEAD
is getting started. The secret of getting started is
BREAKING
your complex, overwhelming
TASKS
into SMALL, MANAGEABLE TASKS,
and then starting on the first one."

Mark Twain

AWESOME AUTHOR OF THE CLASSIC BOOK
ADVENTURES OF HUCKLEBERRY FINN

6.

SMALL STEPS AND GIANT LEAPS

GAINING IN HEIGHT

One of the best ways to improve your performance is to think about any small things—even changes that seem tiny on their own—that could make a **BIG** difference in the long run. These are called **MARGINAL GAINS**, and you'd be amazed what a powerful effect they can have.

Don't believe me? Let's do a little experiment right now. Go find a piece of 8½" × 11" paper. Got it? Now make your best effort at a paper airplane. Then head outside and see how far you can make it fly. Record the distance on the opposite page.

Distance traveled:

....

Once you've noted that down, turn the page to see how marginal
gains can help you make the most **AWESOME** paper airplane ever.

MARGINALLY BETTER

It might surprise you to know that there are people who have dedicated their life's work to figuring out the best method of making paper airplanes. So let's apply some of the things they've discovered to see what a difference marginal gains can make.

EQUIPMENT

Make sure you're using ordinary printer paper, because thicker card stock doesn't fold well. Track down a ruler, scissors, and Scotch tape too.

CONSTRUCTION

Follow the instructions on the next page to make The Stealth version of a paper airplane, excellent for flying long distances. Score the paper with your ruler before folding so the folds are crisp.

THROWING TECHNIQUE

The best way to grip the airplane is between your thumb and forefinger, holding it close to the tip. There are all sorts of fancy throwing techniques you can try, but I recommend the classic overhand.

ENVIRONMENT

If you can, find a large indoor space for your trial. If you have to go outside, try to find somewhere with only a very light breeze.

Now, go and take flight with your paper airplane!

Distance traveled:. . . . .

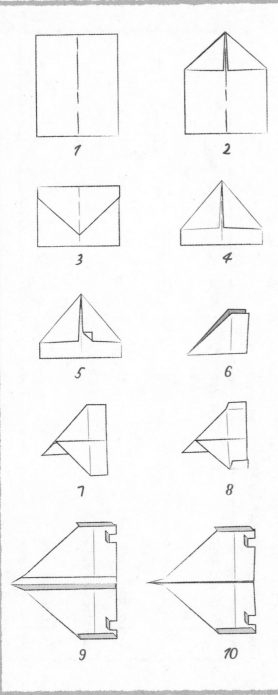

1. Fold the paper in half vertically.

2. Unfold the paper and fold each of the top corners into the center line.

3. Fold the peak toward you, about 0.75 in. from the bottom of the paper.

4. Fold both top corners into the center line, as you did for step two.

5. Fold the remaining tip over the two flaps at the center line to lock them in place.

6. Fold the plane in half vertically.

7. Fold the wings down 1 inch from the bottom of the plane.

8. Fold up the sides of each wing 0.5 inch tall.

9. Cut two small slits at the back of each wing. Fold up the tabs.

10. Make two rings of Scotch tape with the sticky side facing out. Add these to the inside of the body. The finished plane should look like this.

FANTASTIC FINE-TUNING

Making a marginal-gains plan can be a fantastic way of improving your performance overall. Think of an activity that you want to get Awesome at. Then, list all the ways you think marginal gains could help you get there. I've filled out an example plan for you.

STEP 1: Score each Focus Area out of three according to what sort of gain it would give you.

BRAINPOWER GAIN

CONFIDENCE GAIN

SKILL GAIN

STEP 2: Total up your scores. Start by working on the Focus Area with the most points!

I WANT TO GET AWESOME AT: MY FRENCH EXAM

FOCUS AREA	BRAINPOWER GAIN	CONFIDENCE GAIN	SKILL GAIN	TOTAL
Adjust my sleep schedule	3	1	0	4
Listen to French radio	0	2	3	5
Increase meditation	2	1	0	3
Practice with mom	0	3	3	6

I WANT TO GET AWESOME AT:

FOCUS AREA	BRAINPOWER GAIN	CONFIDENCE GAIN	SKILL GAIN	TOTAL

FIND HEADSPACE

Marginal gains don't always involve physical considerations like equipment and diet. Working out how to get yourself into the best space mentally is also really important and can include everything from getting a good night's sleep to listening to the right motivational playlist (or dead silence!) before your big moment.

Imagine you've got a big performance in an assembly coming up. Which mental marginal gains do you think you could apply to make it your best-ever performance?

Get your **HEAD** **IN THE** **GAME**

"YOU
don't have to be
PERFECT
to achieve
YOUR
DREAMS."

Katy Perry
AWESOME SINGER-SONGWRITER

7.
UNDER PRESSURE

LET'S TAKE A BREAK

You don't have to be good at everything. I'm not—remember, I burned breakfast cereal! A growth mindset is about pushing yourself to be the best in areas you really care about—not about trying to be perfect at everything all the time.

Apparently coloring can be really good for helping you relax. So, let's chill out for a bit...and doodle.

THE WORRY JAR

What are the worries that keep you awake at night, or that stress you out when you think about your schoolwork or hobbies? Write them down in the worry jar and note down today's date. Then, in a week's time, come back to this page and see if the same things are bothering you. Cross out the ones that aren't. Who could you talk to about the ones that are still lingering?

DATE:

WORRY JAR

RELAX...

It's important to take time to do things that are fun and relaxing.
Here are some ideas for things to do when life is feeling a bit
overwhelming.

- Go for a walk—take the dog, if you've got one,
  but leave your phone at home.

- Invite some friends over for a pizza and
  movie night.

- Read a book—**NOT** one you have to read for school!

- Make a luxurious cup of hot chocolate (go all
  out with the marshmallows) and savor it.

- Break out a board game on a rainy afternoon.

- Make a playlist of your favorite songs and
  perform your best air guitar in the shower.

THE "CHOKING" CHALLENGE

Often, one of the things that keeps us from trying something new is a fear of choking. I don't mean the type of choking where we try and chomp on so many chocolate cookies that we can't breathe. I mean a fear that we'll freeze in the middle of a really important occasion and screw it up. We've all been there, so let's be up-front about it!

Describe a time when you choked

....

....

....

....

....

How did it make you feel?

....

....

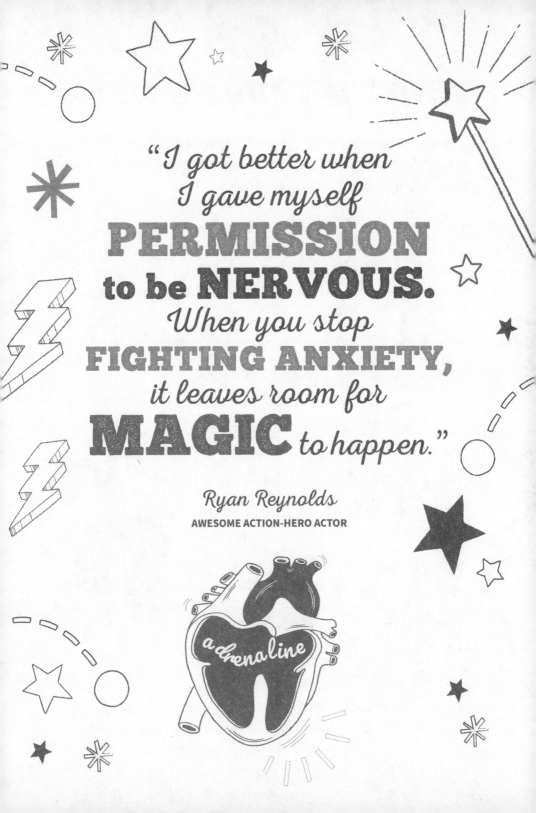

"*I got better when I gave myself* **PERMISSION** *to be* **NERVOUS.** *When you stop* **FIGHTING ANXIETY,** *it leaves room for* **MAGIC** *to happen.*"

Ryan Reynolds
AWESOME ACTION-HERO ACTOR

adrenaline

WHAT'S YOUR PLAN B?

Choking can happen to anyone (it happened to me at the Olympics!), and it's not the end of the world. In fact, there are probably simple steps you can take now to minimize the fallout if you **DO** choke.

Think about a task or event you have coming up. Write down all the things that could go wrong. Then, think about what you would do if those things actually happened. Knowing that you have a **PLAN B** in place takes off a lot of the pressure—and can make it less likely that you'll panic in the first place!

EVENT

COULD GO WRONG

adrenaline

FIX

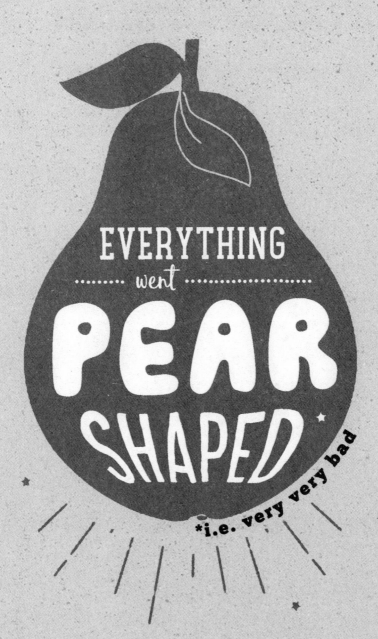

EVERYTHING
.... went ....
PEAR
SHAPED

*i.e. very very bad

STAR BREATHING

If you're feeling anxious, try this simple exercise to keep calm.

Start at any "Breathe in" side, hold your breath at the point, and then breathe out. Keep going until you've gone around the whole star.

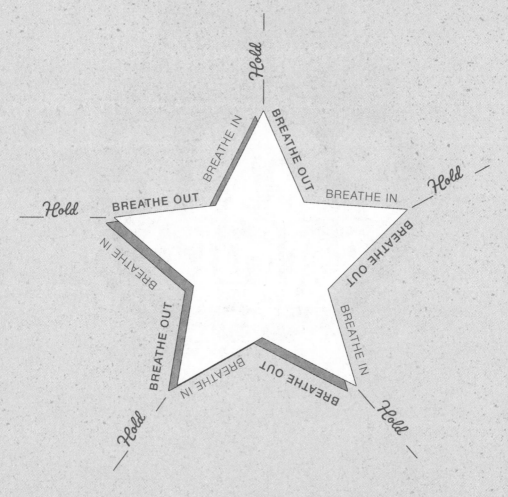

GET GROUNDED...

Another way to stop panic from rising is to ground yourself in your surroundings. Take a deep breath and ...

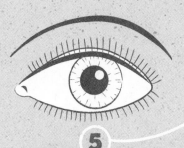

5 *LOOK:* Look around for five things that you can see, and say them out loud.

4 *FEEL:* Pay attention to your body, think of four things that you can feel, and say them out loud. For example, clothes you are wearing or what you are sitting on.

3 *LISTEN:* Listen for three sounds. Say them each out loud.

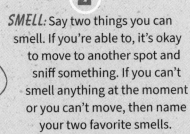

2 *SMELL:* Say two things you can smell. If you're able to, it's okay to move to another spot and sniff something. If you can't smell anything at the moment or you can't move, then name your two favorite smells.

1 *TASTE:* Say one thing you can taste. It may be that morning's toothpaste or the lasagna from lunch. If you can't taste anything, then say your favorite thing to taste.

THE TIME MACHINE TEST

If you're worrying about something you've got to do that's still quite a long way away, try the Time Machine Test.

Let's zoom forward in the time machine to smack-dab in the middle of your big moment. You find that it hasn't gone quite as planned—in fact, it's a **TOTAL DISASTER**. What do you think has caused the epic fail?

° °

° °

° °

° °

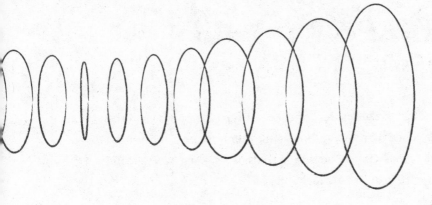

So far this doesn't feel very reassuring, I know. But by picturing the very worst it could get, and why it could have gone so wrong, you can start getting it right. Right **NOW**.

For example, if the reason you think your science presentation will go wrong is because you don't really understand the concepts, you've now got the time to read up, talk to the teacher, and do some practice to really make sure you've got it nailed.

So how can you avoid the failure on the opposite page?

. . . .

. . . .

. . . .

. . . .

That's one fewer thing to worry about, right?

KEEP-IT-COOL CHECKLIST

In the last few pages we've looked at a few different ways you can try and reduce the pressure, both in the moment and in the run-up. Think of all of these as your anxiety checklist, something for you to run through if it all starts to feel a bit much.

IN THE LONG TERM

- Try to figure out what's bothering you with the **Worry Jar**. You could even make an actual worry jar from a container and fill it with worries written on scraps of paper.

- Take the **Time Machine Test**. Do it far in advance so you have plenty of time to make sure a big event goes as smoothly as possible.

IN THE MEDIUM TERM

- **Relax!** When you're feeling stressed, sometimes the best way to remedy it is to take a break and look after yourself. Go and do something fun, completely guilt-free.

- Think about your **Plan Bs**. These are quick-fix solutions you can put in place in case you choke during your big moment.

WHEN THE SPOTLIGHT'S ON YOU

○ If you're just about to get underway and you're feeling panicked, do some **Star Breathing**. It's amazing what a difference it can make!

○ Don't forget to **Get Grounded**. Reminding yourself of your surroundings will help you to stay calm.

"*I was* **TAUGHT** *that the way of* **PROGRESS** *was* **NEITHER** **SWIFT** *nor* **EASY.**"

Marie Curie

AWESOME SCIENTIST AND WINNER OF TWO NOBEL PRIZES

8.

DON'T STOP ME NOW

TOP 10 GROWTH MINDSET QUESTIONS

Let's remind ourselves of the important points about growth mindset. Challenging yourself is important, and so is believing you can achieve your goals and trusting your brain to help you get better at something each time you practice it, even if you make mistakes sometimes. Remembering all of this is what will help you develop your growth mindset. So, try and ask yourself these questions at least once a week.

1 What did you try hard at today?

2 What made you keep going?

3 Were you frightened of failing today?

4 Did that hold you back from trying something new?

5 What mistake did you make that you learned from?

6 What will you do to improve your schoolwork tomorrow?

7 How did you make your practice harder today?

8 What will you do to get better at your favorite hobby?

9 What obstacle did you encounter today?

10 What will you do to overcome it?

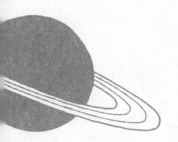 

YOUR GROWTH MINDSET MANTRA

If you start to feel those old doubts and fixed mindset thoughts creep in when you think about your goal, repeat this growth mindset mantra to yourself every day.

I'm going to
PRACTICE HARD.

I'm going to
STICK WITH IT.

I'm going to be
POSITIVE ABOUT IT

and I'm really
PROUD OF IT!

MY AWESOME REMINDER

And if that's not enough, then complete this page and keep coming back
to it whenever your self-confidence could use a boost!

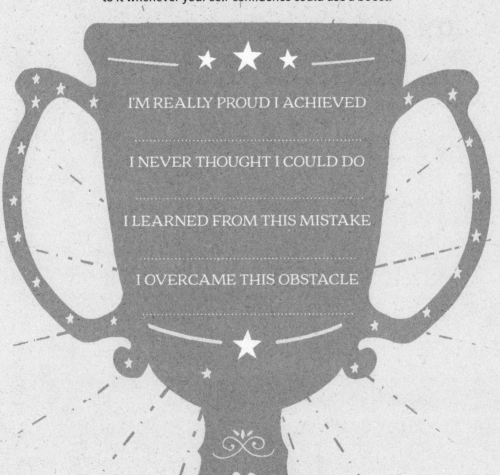

I'M REALLY PROUD I ACHIEVED

I NEVER THOUGHT I COULD DO

I LEARNED FROM THIS MISTAKE

I OVERCAME THIS OBSTACLE

GET INSPIRED

Here are three more Awesome achievers who inspire me to work hard and dream big.

MICHELLE OBAMA

Michelle grew up on the South Side of Chicago, where her parents rented a small apartment. When her beloved father developed multiple sclerosis, Michelle felt that the best thing she could do was to work hard and make him proud. She was a determined girl and was accepted at a prestigious, selective school. The round trip from her home to school on the other side of the city took three hours. Michelle was anxious about how she would be perceived by the other students, but she managed to ignore any negative comments and used them as fuel to keep her going. Her high school teachers advised her against applying to Princeton University, but she was accepted there and to Harvard. She went on to become a highly successful lawyer and then the First Lady of the United States.

Appetite FOR HARD WORK

JESSICA ENNIS-HILL

Jessica Ennis-Hill, a British track-and-field athlete, was already competing in international events by 2007, but she suffered an injury that forced her to miss out on the 2008 Olympics. Determined not to let failure stop her, Jessica proved her resilience by working harder than ever to recover, winning gold at the 2012 London Olympics and silver in Rio in 2016.

MUHAMMAD ALI

When a thief stole Muhammad's bike and he flew into a rage, a police officer suggested Muhammad put his energy into boxing. And Muhammad did—he trained with a fervor that was unmatched by any other boy in the ring. He won 100 amateur fights and an Olympic gold medal before going professional. Muhammad was suspended from boxing when he refused to fight in the Vietnam War because of his religious beliefs, but he used it as an opportunity to develop his public-speaking skills and speak out against racism. When the ban was lifted three years later, Muhammad used his resilience and determination to get back to the top, fighting the world's best heavyweight boxers to prove he was the greatest.

YOUR GROWTH MINDSET TOOLBOX

If you've made it this far through the book, it's fair to say you are well on your way to being a Growth Mindset Yoda! You've got your goals in mind and a plan for how you're going to achieve them.

There are **SO** many things from this book that you can use to help get you there. Just remember, you've got all of these tools in your growth mindset tool kit.

Growth Mindset Mantra

Mistakes Diary

S-T-R-E-T-C-H
Y-O-U-R-S-E-L-F

AWESOME CREW

FREE UP YOUR BRAIN

KEEP-IT-COOL CHECKLIST

Fantastic Fine-Tuning

Are there any other tools you can think of?

CONCLUSION

Phew! There is a lot to do and think about in this journal. And I meant it at the beginning when I said that whether you do all of it, some of it, or even just one thing,

the IMPORTANT thing is that you START.

And by now you have read *You Are Awesome*, right? Surely? You must have? You can't still be missing out on what I've been told is the most epic book since Shakespeare wrote that one about the boyfriend and girlfriend? Okay, okay, that was my mom again.

If you still haven't read it, then you're making me cry into my (burnt) breakfast cereal. So, I'm going to dry my eyes, throw away the charcoal-flakes, and just make sure we're all clear and all set to move forward with our **Awesome** journey.

So, here are your **YOU ARE AWESOME** takeaways (the things you should remember even if everything goes flying out of your brain as soon as you start thinking of the pepperoni pizza you'll be eating for dinner).

1. **SUCCESS**—you're not born with a gold medal on your chest. That isn't how success happens. It is a journey with a lot of hard work, determination, and obstacles along the way.

2. **COMFORT ZONE**—get out of it. Because when it comes to achieving your goals, if you don't, then you definitely won't.

3. **PRACTICE**—do it the hard way. The easy stuff is not going to be enough to change the game.

4. **FAILURE**—get used to it. You're going to make mistakes. Make sure you use them positively and learn everything you can from them. And, **SPOILER ALERT**…everyone else is making them too, even if they're not telling you about them.

5. And finally…**RELAX**. Seriously, don't forget to chill out sometimes. Yes, there may be a lot to do, but don't feel like you need to do it all at once.

And remember, this journal is here to help you. Everyone needs a little help to achieve their goals, and there are lots of people around you who will be happy to help you if you have the courage to ask.

When I was nineteen, I qualified to play in the Under-20s U.S. Open Table Tennis Championship. I wasn't expected to make the cut, so it was all a bit of a shock, but I had practiced really hard and I'd achieved something I hadn't dared to believe was possible. So I was wildly excited. I'd practically finished packing my suitcase before I'd showered from the qualifying match.

And then the reality set in. My mom and dad didn't have the money for fancy flights to the USA. That was the whole reason I'd had to take a twenty-four-hour bus to practice in Norway in the first place (we weren't able to afford the flight and the whole Germany mix-up started right there).

So that was it. Back to the gym in Reading. In despair that my American dream was over before it had even begun. That was until… my Awesome Crew stepped in. Brian Halliday, Jimmy Stokes, John Glew, and many, many others from the streets near my house in Reading decided to donate their own actual money so I could go to play in Baltimore. And let's not get the wrong idea here—these guys were not like Bill Gates or Richard Branson. They didn't have millions in the bank. No, they were just Awesome people who were super keen to help me fulfill my potential.

It was the trip of a lifetime. And I was determined to be my absolute best. If these guys could sacrifice their money, then I was going to make sure I was in the very best form I could be when I got out to the table and played the tournament. And I won it. I won the whole tournament. I was the Under-20s U.S. Open Champion!

I owe that Awesome Crew much more than money. Much more than they will ever know. I owe them a huge debt for their belief in me and their willingness to give me the opportunity to achieve my dream. A dream that opened my eyes to the possibilities that lay ahead.

There are so many amazing people out there. Teachers, coaches, family, friends. Learn from them. Recruit them into your Awesome Crew. They'll want to help you. Why? Because…

YOU ARE AWESOME!

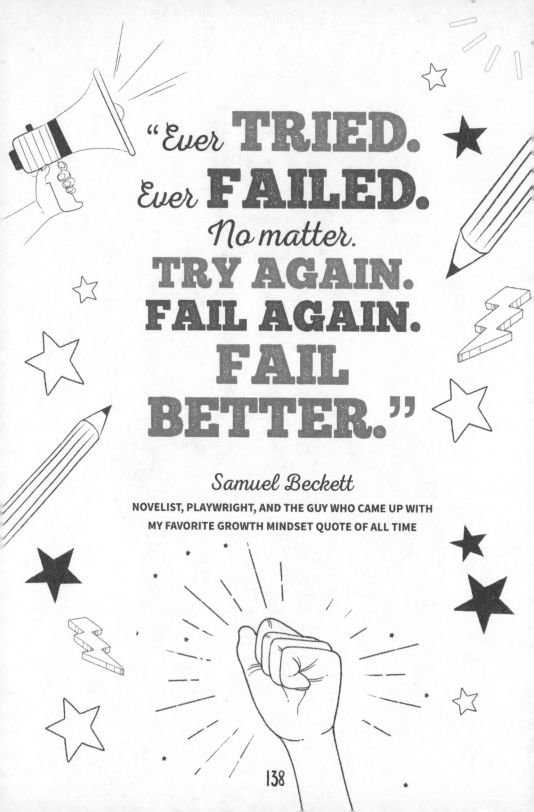

"*Ever* **TRIED.** *Ever* **FAILED.** *No matter.* **TRY AGAIN. FAIL AGAIN. FAIL BETTER."**

Samuel Beckett

NOVELIST, PLAYWRIGHT, AND THE GUY WHO CAME UP WITH MY FAVORITE GROWTH MINDSET QUOTE OF ALL TIME

MY AWESOME NOTES

_____

_____

_____

_____

_____

_____

_____

_____

MY AWESOME NOTES

_____

_____

_____

_____

_____

_____

_____

_____

_____

_____

_____

_____

_____

_____

_____

_____

_____

_____

_____

_____

_____

_____

_____

REFERENCES

In order of appearance

MICHELLE OBAMA

Obama, Michelle. "A Passionate, Personal Case for Education." Filmed April 2009 in London. Elizabeth G. Anderson School video, 11:33, accessed June 30, 2018. https://www.ted.com/talks/michelle_obama/transcript.

VINCENT VAN GOGH

van Gogh, Vincent. Vincent van Gogh to Anthon van Rappard, August 18, 1885. *Vincent van Gogh: The Letters*, no. 528. http://www.vangoghletters.org/vg/letters/let528/letter.html#translation.

ALBERT EINSTEIN

Mayer, Jerry and John P. Holms, comps. *Bite-Size Einstein: Quotations on Just About Everything from the Greatest Mind of the Twentieth Century*. New York: St. Martin's Press, 1996.

JESSE JACKSON

Fiske, Edward B. "Jesse Jackson Builds Up Support In a Drive for Student Discipline." *New York Times*, March 4, 1979 (reported spoken statement). https://www.nytimes.com/1979/03/04/archives/jesse-jackson-builds-up-support-in-a-drive-for-student-discipline.html.

MICHAEL PHELPS

Phelps, Michael. *No Limits: The Will to Succeed*. London: Simon & Schuster, 2009.

OPRAH WINFREY

Winfrey, Oprah. "Go For It!" *O, The Oprah Magazine*, September 2003.

THE FORGETTING CURVE

Ebbinghaus, Hermann. *Memory: A Contribution to Experimental Psychology*. Translated by Henry A. Ruger and Clara E. Bussenius. New York: Columbia University, 1913.

THOMAS EDISON

Rosanoff, Martin André. "Edison in His Laboratory." *Harper's Magazine*, September 1932 (reported spoken statement, c. 1902).

J.K. ROWLING

Rowling, J.K. "The Fringe Benefits of Failure." Filmed June 2008 in Cambridge, MA. Harvard University video, 20:58, accessed June 30, 2018. https://www.ted.com/talks/jk_rowling_the_fringe_benefits_of_failure.

JUSTIN TIMBERLAKE

Timberlake, Justin. Interview by Oprah Winfrey. *Oprah's Master Class*. OWN: Oprah Winfrey Network, May 11, 2014 (television interview).

MARK TWAIN

Mason, Felicia. "Break Down Big Jobs to Help Build Your Life." *Daily Press* (Newport News, VA), September 25, 1997 (reported spoken statement).

PAPER AIRPLANE

Henderson, Sam. "How to Make a Paper Airplane." DIY Network. Accessed July 18, 2019. https://www.diynetwork.com/made-and-remade/learn-it/5-basic-paper-airplanes.

KATY PERRY

Hauser, Brooke. "Katy Perry Celebrates Her Independence." *Parade*, June 28, 2012 (magazine interview). https://parade.com/31418/brookehauser/28-katy-perry-part-of-me/.

RYAN REYNOLDS

Reynolds, Ryan (@VancityReynolds). "Embrace it. I got better when I gave myself permission to be nervous." Twitter, June 18, 2018. https://twitter.com/i/web/status/1008785587824971776.

MARIE CURIE

Curie, Marie. *Pierre Curie with Autobiographical Notes by Marie Curie*. New York: Macmillan, 1923.

SAMUEL BECKETT

Beckett, Samuel. "Worstword Ho." *Nohow On*. New York: Grove Press, 1989.